All My Angel Friends

Written & Illustrated

by Leia A. Stinnett

Other Books by Leia Stinnett:

A Circle of Angels
The Twelve Universal Laws

The Little Angel Books Series:

The Angel Told Me to Tell You Good-bye
The Bridge Between Two Worlds
Color Me One
Crystals R for Kids
Exploring the Chakras
Happy Feet
One Red Rose
When the Earth Was New
Where Is God?
Who's Afraid of the Dark?

Cover art
by Leia Stinnett

ISBN 0-929385-80-2
Published by
Light Technology Publishing
P.O. Box 1526, Sedona, AZ 86339
(520) 282-6523

Printed by
MISSION POSSIBLE
Commercial
Printing
P.O. Box 1495
Sedona, AZ 86339

All My Angel Friends

This very special book has been lovingly designed by all our angel friends so that while you color the many beautiful angel pictures, you will learn about the different ways in which the angelic kingdom helps each of us here on Earth.

Angels want us to know they love and care about us as they do the plant, animal and mineral worlds, even the entire universe. Although angels have been given specific jobs to do, they share with each other the many tasks in the heavens and on this planet so all of creation stays in balance and harmony.

It is important for each of us to be aware of the beautiful angels who love and care for us and to be thankful for all the wonderful things they help us learn about ourselves and the Earth school. Angels want us to be happy, healthy and loving, just as they are. They work very hard to help us see love and goodness in ourselves and each other.

The angels hope you enjoy learning about them in this little book they have helped prepare. They also would like you to feel comfortable in asking them for guidance and protection, or in calling on them at any time you want to be with a very special friend who loves you unconditionally.

Drawings, paintings and sculptures from long ago in many different civilizations depict angels as having a human form, wearing long robes, having wings at their shoulder area and displaying a large ring of light, or ***halo***, around their heads. We must ask ourselves, however, is this really how angels look or is this just one way we see them in our mind?

Angels are pure energy of unconditional love and joy. They do not have a body as we do because their ***energy vibrations*** are much higher than ours, as is light. Their energy patterns can appear to us as though they have wings, and they can come to us as colored balls of light that we can see in our ***inner vision***.

These beautiful forms of energy have been created by God to assist all of creation in spiritual awakening and evolution. As we each come to the Earth school to learn our lessons of choice, certain angels are assigned to assist us in awakening to all our great gifts of self-healing, inner knowing and vision, creating a harmonious,

FROM GOD
TO: TONY

joyful life, choosing loving relationships and more.

Great numbers of angels exist, each having a specific job to do. This little book will help you better understand how your angel friends can help you grow spiritually and be more loving and happy.

ANGELS SERVE AS GOD'S MESSENGERS

Sometimes we do not listen to our inner voice and we might find ourselves struggling with our Earth lessons. To assist us God might send an angelic messenger to help us realize what we need to do to change the situation. This messenger might inform us of a special event about to take place in our life so we will not be uncomfortable when it occurs or how to deal with a challenge, a difficult lesson, a friend, so that the end result will be a positive one.

Angels might speak to us in our dreams, in a vision we see in our mind's eye, through a friend, a teacher or a book we read, through our own inner knowing or thoughts. If we are open to all

possibilities and listen carefully to all messages we receive, no matter how ridiculous they might seem to others or even to ourselves, we can save ourselves from a very negative experience.

Angelic messengers bring us news to help us feel safe, happy and loved.

THE GUARDIAN ANGELS

Have you ever been in a situation where you could have hurt yourself and someone or something seemed to push you out of the way just in time? Have you ever fallen and suddenly found yourself lying on the ground, unhurt, feeling like you just landed on a soft, fluffy cloud.

Perhaps it is time to acknowledge and thank a very special, loving friend – your guardian angel. This special angel has been assigned to watch over you from the moment of your birth, throughout your entire life experience, until the moment you leave this world to pass on to the world of spirit.

Your guardian angel is responsible for keeping you safe from harm. You can feel this angel's warnings in the pit of your stomach: "No, you had better not do that. It doesn't feel right!" Or, you might hear a voice in

your inner ear, or in your mind warning you of a situation that might not be good for you. The angel will never tell you what to do or how to do it, but he/she will be there to protect you in your experiences and will try very hard to encourage you to make positive choices.

While you sleep at night, your guardian angel is right there at your bedside to help make you feel safe. If you listen carefully you might even hear the angel singing a special lullaby.

ANGELS HELP US HEAL OURSELVES

Angels are very loving, happy beings of light. They want us to be happy as well; however, it is often difficult for us to be happy when we are not feeling well.

Any time we are not feeling well, we can simply ask our healing angels to give us a hand. These angels will serve as a pipeline from God to us and back to God. They draw light from God, help us project it to the part of us that is out of balance and then reflect the negative energy causing our discomfort back to God where it is recycled into love and light.

When you are not feeling well, ask the angels of healing to send their light-love energy into your body. You will feel heat and/or tingling energy moving into your body, helping that part of you that does not feel well come into balance. You can then place your own hands on that part of your body that does not feel well. Let the angels pass their loving energy through your

hands and into your body. When you feel the process is complete, thank the angels for their loving support. Remove your hands. You will feel wonderfully energized and balanced.

Healing angels can help you heal plants and animals as well, and will also assist you in sending loving, healing energy out over the entire Earth.

ANGELS ARE ALWAYS SUPPORTIVE

No matter how we are feeling or what we are needing, the angels are always anxious to help. They want us to be happy and healthy as we learn in the Earth school. Talk to the angels. Treat them like your very best friends. When you do, you will never feel lonely or unloved, because they are always there for each of us. Keep a special notebook of your sharings with the angels so you can see the many ways they offer help.

ANGELS OFFER SPIRITUAL GUIDANCE

In our spiritual growth there might be times when we have questions for which answers are difficult to find. We can call upon the angels who love us to guide us to a special book or teacher.

Angels are experts at helping us find just the right answers to any spiritual challenge, as they want us to continue to grow in God's light easily and effortlessly. These angels help us tune in to our intuition and find our own answers, rather than depending on others to tell us what to do and how to do it. They remind us that only each individual knows what is right for him/herself. It is important to follow one's own truth.

Many of us cannot *see* angels, but we still know they are near. How do we know our angels are close by?

- Often you might feel a very strong sense of love, like someone just put their arms around you and gave you a great big hug. The entire room might feel loving, warm, as though there is a beautiful glow about it. It will feel safe and happy.
- You might *see* your angel in a

TOO MUCH
TOO LITTLE
MY TRUTH
=
BALANCE
JUST RIGHT

form similar to our own body, as moving energy or as colored balls or streaks of light shooting by. You might feel someone near and see something out of the corner of your eye, but when you turn, no one seems to be there. The angels are with you all the time. You can sense or feel their presence whether you actually see them or not. They might even make a noise to let you know they are there.

• Sometimes you might wonder about something you are questioning as to whether it is true or not. And then a chill goes up your spine, your arm, your whole body. The angel has touched your energy body to give you a sign that what you are thinking or feeling is true. Your heart signals truth; your stomach signals things that are not true. Pay attention to your body.

• Sometimes you might hear a buzzing sound, a tone or a musical note in your ear. This is your angel communicating with you. You can hear energy when you are very still. You might hear the angels speak in words or just *know* (as thoughts in your mind) what they are saying.

• You might smell some wonderful fragrance as though you are standing in a field of roses, jasmine, lilacs or some other flowers. This special fragrance might be a sign of a very special angel guide. Other people might not even smell this fragrance because their angels have a different smell about them. If your friends do smell the fragrance, you can bet they will ask where that beautiful smell is coming from.

THE NINE ANGEL GROUPS

There are nine different groups of angels, each having a very specific job, with each job equally important as the next. Without one group of angels, a very important job might not get done.

The Seraphim, Cherubim and Throne Angels have a very high vibration and are at a level of service closer to God than the other groupings of angels.

The Dominions, Virtues and Powers act as a bridge between the heavens and the Earth, in many ways helping us realize that God is in all things and in each of us equally.

The Principalities, Archangels and Angels are the grouping of angelic beings who work most closely with we humans experiencing the Earth school.

The **Seraphim Angels** (pronounced *Sara-fim*) are the angels closest to God's "throne" in the heavens. These angels send out beautiful waves of divine love all over the universe helping us always remember how much God loves us. Any time we feel that we are not loved or appreciated, we can call upon the Seraphim who will help us move all the unloving energy out of our way.

The **Cherubim Angels** are the caretakers of wisdom. Whenever we

THE
OTHER
←PATH
TO→
GOD

need help with a situation or an answer to a challenge that we are faced with in life, we can call upon the Cherubim to help us access God's wisdom. There is no challenge too large or too small for this group of angels. They are always there and happy to assist us.

The **Thrones** remind us to have more faith, to trust more in ourselves and our inner knowing, and to make wise decisions about our life experiences so we do not have the same experiences over and over, or be unhappy. These angels are very special because they help us follow God's path even when our friends or other people try to make us follow their paths.

The **Dominions** are the "planners" of the heavens. When we struggle and try to control our lives, to make things happen, we often meet challenges and difficulties along the way. The Dominions are there to help us plan our life in a positive, loving way. As we surrender to God and seek God's help in moving to the next step in our spiritual growth, the Dominions are right there to prepare the way.

The **Virtues** are the miracle workers. You might say, "Why, that's a miracle. I didn't get hurt!" You can thank the Virtue Angels for assisting you to safety. They love you and want you to be safe.

The **Powers** are in charge of God's Universal Law of cause and effect. These angels teach us that when we are experiencing a lot of negativity in our life we must look within ourselves. Are we unhappy? Are we angry? The Powers show us that by healing our own negative thoughts, feelings and emotions, we will draw more happy, loving friends into our lives. We will be happy.

The **Principalities** rule nations, provinces and countries of the world. Their job is to protect religious and world leaders and to help these leaders make important decisions that will benefit their country and the world. If you feel the president of your country, or the leader of your church or school needs assistance, call upon the Principalities to assist.

ARCHANGEL MICHAEL
ARCHAII FAITH

The male and female angelic leaders of thousands of angels, the ***Archangels*** and ***Archaii***, act as bridges or go-betweens to help us understand and work with God's universal truths.

Archangel Michael and **Archaii Faith** teach us the correct use of power. They share with us the importance of standing in our own power, not letting others control us, and not trying to control other people to benefit ourselves. Michael and Faith offer us protection from unloving energies and teach us to have faith that when we ask, we will have everything we require to be happy and healthy.

Archangel Gabriel and **Archaii Hope** teach us the importance of forgiving everyone and everything in our past so we can continue to grow spiritually. They help us understand that thinking about the past all the time keeps us feeling stuck in the same place. When it is time for us to pass from our physical form to spirit form, or light, these special angels are at our side to help us move on lovingly.

Archangel Uriel and **Archaii Donna Grace** encourage us to be selfless, to lovingly offer help to others without expecting

WHILE HELPING US, ANGELS LEARN
MANY LESSONS ABOUT THE EARTH SCHOOL.

anything in return. Remember, when you give unselfishly from your heart, you get a lot more good things in return.

Archangel Raphael and **Archaii Mother Mary** share with us ways we can heal ourselves and see things more clearly from our inner vision.

Archangel Jophiel and **Archaii Constance** help us realize the importance of God's wisdom and love in our everyday lives and to pay attention to this love rather than some of the negative things we feel and see in the material world.

Archangel Chamuel and **Archaii Charity** remind us daily to think, feel and do things from our heart, from divine love.

Archangel Zadkiel and **Holy Amethyst** help us have compassion for other people, even for those who have hurt us in some way.

LOVE

LET'S MEET YOUR ANGEL

Sit quietly in a chair or on the floor where you will not be disturbed. Close your eyes and breathe very deeply, allowing your body to relax as you breathe. Ask God to protect you in His/Her beautiful white light. Imagine you are moving up above the clouds surrounded in God's protective shield of light, moving up into the beautiful world of the angels.

Ask your special guardian angel to come closer where you can see or feel him or her. As your angel comes near you will feel warm, loving energy—a feeling of peace. You will feel very safe, for this angel has come to be with you from the time you are born until you return to God. His or her job is to protect you, to keep you safe, to help you when you feel afraid or that you cannot achieve your goals.

With your mind's eye you might feel and see colors—soft pastel colors that tell you your angel is near.

When you feel or see your angel, think about your angel

and ask him/her to give you a name. Listen very carefully. Some angels have names like ours – Sara, John, Ann, Paul. Other angels have very different names – Jo-El, Ra-Ya-El and so on. Sometimes the angel does not have a name but will help you hear a sound or see a color. It is not important to have a name but to know through feelings that your very special guardian angel is close by.

Listen to the angel's message if he or she has something to say to you. You might hear a voice or just hear thoughts in your mind. You must be very quiet to really hear what the angel has to say.

Now thank your angel for visiting you and send him or her lots of love from your heart. Anytime you want your angel near just think about him or her. It's easy.

Each angel of the angelic kingdom has a specific job to do in serving us on planet Earth. Angels represent all that is good, true and beautiful. When we communicate with and connect to the angel's higher vibrations, we will experience all good things in our lives.

In meeting the angels you will notice they do not always appear in the same form and shape. There are times you might see only a dim outline of energy; they can change from a shining ball of light to a form resembling our own and into a shape or symbol such as a cube, a triangle, a circle and so on.

The angels listed on the following pages have specific jobs to do in helping us grow in God's light. Call upon the angel who works with the area of your life you are most concerned

GOD + ME =
LOVE

with. If you do not know which angel to call upon, simply ask the appropriate angel to step forward so you can discuss your situation with them.

Talk to the angels just as you would your parents, teachers or friends, for truly the angels love and care about you more than you might realize. Angels are your very best friends.

The **Angels of Karma** help us realize that Earth is a school in which we are each responsible for our own actions. These angels work directly with us to help us better understand the law of karma so we do not have to experience the same lesson over and over again. They help us master our thoughts, feelings, words and deeds so we can move easily through our earthly experiences as we evolve spiritually.

Guardian Angels are God's gift to us when we

HATE
SORROW
ANGER
JUDGMENT
GUILT
LOVE
JOY
LOVE
JOY
PEACE

are born. These angels protect us, guide us and help us achieve our goals as we move through this life experience.

Angels of Spiritual Fire are the keepers of the spiritual flames, which consist of every color of the rainbow: red, orange, yellow, green, blue, violet, as well as blue-green, magenta, gold, peach and opal. These angels help us better understand the importance of changing negative energy to positive, loving energy and will share with us through meditation how to work with the flame to do just that.

Solar Angels help us realize we are one with God and assist us in attuning to God's higher vibrations, thus creating for ourselves perfect health, eternal youth, beauty, joy, abundance and so on.

The **Angel of Abundance –** Money is a big lesson for many of us here on Earth. It is the greatest test of our ability to be free.

We often believe we are limited by how much money we have to spend. People are often judged to be very powerful because they have a lot of money and possessions. In God's kingdom we are each equally abundant. Many of us, however, do not feel abundant or think we deserve to be abundant. But the truth is that whatever we ask for we will receive when we *know* we deserve it. This angel will help each of us experience abundance as we experience our lessons here on Earth.

Angel of Creative Wisdom— This special angel helps us get in touch with our inner guidance and learn to follow our own intuition. We can test ourselves in our ability to follow our inner guidance by examining the results of situations when we do follow our guidance and when we do not. This angel will help us solve our problems easily and quickly by helping us work from that place of our higher self – a place that is always drawing from the wisdom of God rather than from what other people think or feel here on Earth.

The **Angel of Victory** helps us meet our goals and be proud of all our accomplishments no matter how large or small they might seem to us. "There is no such thing as failure," states this angel, "unless you never try.

Every achievement is an important one."

The **Angel of Order and Harmony** helps us stay centered and balanced without judging one another or taking sides. With this angel's help we can see the whole picture – the truth. As we see the truth in all things, we can then help others see their truth as well.

The **Angel of Discernment** says, "Look at all situations very carefully." Ask yourself, Have I learned this lesson already? Or, If I get involved, will I get hurt in some way? If you have already learned the lesson, or if you feel the experience will be an unhappy one for you, walk away. Discernment, or seeing all things clearly is a very important lesson, helping us move through our lessons with fewer challenges.

The **Angel of Cycles** says, "Expect the unexpected. Expect change. Everything in the universe is constantly changing and moving. When we are willing to make changes in our life, we grow spiritually. Be open to all situations. React to every situation from a loving space and be willing to move from one experience to another."

ANGELS WATCH OVER THE ANIMAL KINGDOM . . .

. . . AND THE PLANT KINGDOM . . .

. . . AND THE MINERAL KINGDOM, TOO!

ANGELS LOVE TO PROTECT THE ENVIRONMENT.

. . . AND KEEP OUR WATERWAYS FRESH AND CLEAR,
SAFE FOR US TO DRINK.

ANGELS HELP REGULATE OUR RAINFALL . . .

. . . AND ANGELS HELP US WITH OUR MUSIC LESSONS.

WE ARE NOT HERE TO JUDGE OTHERS AS RIGHT OR WRONG, BUT WE DO NOT HAVE TO JOIN INTO A SITUATION WE ARE NOT COMFORTABLE WITH.

The **Angel of Unconditional Love and Freedom** teaches us not to judge or criticize others, whether or not we feel they are doing what is right. "Love all of creation as you love God. Love yourself as you love God. Do not judge others, but have love and compassion for them. Through love and compassion all negative thoughts, feelings and emotions can be healed and balanced. The more love you share with others, the more love will come back to you. God is love and God loves each of us equally, all the time."

The **Angel of Illusions and Reality** says that while we are learning in the Earth school it is important for us to see what is real and what is not real. Things that are not real are called ***illusions***.

This angel helps us feel closer to God and God's plan and less connected to what is here for us to experience on Earth. This angel says, "Do not worry about the future, but remember you create your own future and can change whatever you are afraid of or do not want to experience."

Part of our lessons here on Earth is to learn to see through the illusions of limitations ("I can't do that because..."), structure ("I can't break the rules..."), feeling helpless and so on. As we learn what is real we move closer to God.

JOY
LOVE
PEACE

The **Angel of Power and Authority** reminds us that because we are one with God we, too, have a divine, or God-given power, to create love, happiness and joy in our world.

We are not in control here on Earth. We might think we are, but the more we try to "make" things happen, the more we try to control other people, the more unhappy we become. As we surrender to God and have faith that whatever we need and ask for will come to us, our life begins to flow smoothly and happily.

The **Angel of Spiritual Understanding** helps us be more God-like – thinking, speaking and doing things from our hearts, from love. Through this angel's teachings we learn that our conscious mind, or physical mind, can lead us into situations that make us uncomfortable and unhappy, while our God-mind, our higher self, always guides us lovingly

I LOVE MYSELF
I LOVE GOD
GOD LOVES YOU
LOVE

and joyfully from one lesson to another.

The **Angel of Loving Relationships** offers, "You deserve to have great friends, friends who will respect you and share things with you rather than selfish, hurtful friends."

As we become more loving ourselves, we send out that loving energy to the world like a radio signal, telling other loving people we would like to have them as friends. If you want happy, loving friends, be happy and loving yourself.

The **Angel of Patience and Acceptance** helps us see the importance of thinking and doing things we need to do only in this moment. This angel says, "You do not have to experience unhappy things or fear the future. Remember, you can create your own future. What you think about *you* make happen. God loves us all and wants us to be happy. People, not God, create problems for themselves from what they think or believe. Think loving, positive things; create loving, positive things."

The **Angel of Materiality and Temptation** helps us feel connected to the Earth as we grow spiritually. This angel teaches us that God and our spiritual growth is

what is really important and that the material things we have here on Earth cannot bring us the happiness and love that God does. This angel points out that everything we have on Earth is only borrowed and that we will not be taking our things with us when we go back to spirit.

The **Angel of Courage and Perseverance** supports us when we feel we need to follow our own truth rather than what other people want us to do. This angel also shares that we cannot change other people. We are not responsible for their happiness and well-being. We are not here to judge other people or blame others, for then we are judging and blaming ourselves because we are all part of God.

We can agree to be the best that we can be and through our own positive changes, by example, we can help other people change and be more loving as well.

The **Angel of Spiritual Strength and Will** says, "Hang in there on your spiritual path, even when you feel stuck or when others challenge you. When you listen to your inner voice and follow what you feel is right rather than what others tell you to do, you will always find your life moving in the right direction, following God's plan. When you follow your heart, you will learn your lessons easily and joyfully.

The **Angel of Renunciation and Regeneration** lovingly reminds us, "Your spiritual path is very important, for this is the path to joy, happiness, love and fulfillment. When you spend more time being concerned about material things, you can feel separate from God, unhappy or worried that something might happen to your things. Always remember that you cannot take your things with you when you leave your body to return to God.

The **Angel of Death and Rebirth** helps with the birth of a child, making it feel comfortable and loved as it comes into the physical world. This angel is also helpful to people choosing to leave the earthly experience through the process of death. When we die we simply leave our physical body of this life experience and return to God, only to be given another opportunity to return to Earth to experience new lessons.

You might call this angel the "recycler of souls."

The **Angel of Service** helps us learn the reason we have come to Earth as God's helpers. This angel helps us learn how we can serve God by helping other people as a healer, a teacher or a spiritual leader.

The **Angel of Imagination and Freedom** helps us use our ***inner vision*** to see people, things and situations as they really are. In this way we learn what is real according to God's laws and what is illusion according to the rules humankind has created to control others.

The **Angel of Truth** helps us know we are one with God . . . not separate from God. Through this angel's teaching we learn to understand and work with our special gifts from God such as our intuition and our ability to heal ourself, or how to create what we need to be happy on Earth.

The **Angel of Creative Word** teaches us that whatever we think, say or do affects all living things. As we learn to care for and love ourselves we share those feelings with all living things. When we love ourselves we love other people as well.

The **Angel of Success** helps us overcome feelings of failure or of not being good enough to reach our goals. "Believe in yourself," this angel tells us. "Success comes to each of us who accepts God as part of us and that through our God-given gifts we can achieve our goals easily and effortlessly."

ANGELS HELP US GO TO THE WORLD OF SPIRIT
TO BE BORN AGAIN.

ANGELS DO HAVE TIME TO PLAY AND REST.

ABOUT THE AUTHOR

The '80s were a decade of self-discovery for Leia Stinnett after she began researching many different avenues of spirituality. In her profession as a graphic designer she had become restless, knowing there was something important she had to do outside the materiality of corporate America.

In August 1986 Leia had her first contact with Archangel Michael when he appeared in a physical form of glowing blue light. A voice said, "I am Michael. Together we will save the children."

In 1988 she was inspired by Michael to teach spiritual classes in Sacramento, California, the Circle of Angels. Through these classes she had the opportunity to work with learning-disabled children, children of abuse and those from dysfunctional homes.

Later Michael told her, "Together we are going to write the Little Angel Books." To date Leia and Michael have created thirteen Little Angel Books that present various topics of spiritual truths and principles. The books proved popular among adults as well as children.

The Circle of Angels classes have been introduced to several countries around the world and across the U.S., and Leia and her husband Douglas now have a teacher's manual and training program for people who wish to offer spiritual classes to children. Leia and Michael have been interviewed on Canadian Satellite TV and have appeared on NBC-TV's *Angels II – Beyond the Light*, which featured their Circle of Angels class and discussed their books and Michael's visit.

The angels have given Leia and Douglas a vision of a new educational system without competition or grades – one that supports love and positive self-esteem, honoring all children as the independent lights they are. Thus they are now writing a curriculum for the new "schools of light" and developing additional books and programs for children.